T0316621

FOR THE DURATION

❧ Poems ❦

Jana van Niekerk
Rosemund Handler
Natalie Railoun

Published by
Botsotso
Box 30952
Braamfontein, 2017

botsotso@artslink.co.za
www.botsotso.org.za

©in the text: the poets themselves 2015

Cover, layout, design: Chimurengalab

ISBN: 978-0-9814205-5-4

We would like to thank the National Arts Council of South Africa
for its assistance in publishing this book.

NATIONAL ARTS COUNCIL
OF SOUTH AFRICA

an agency of the
Department of Arts and Culture

Image credits

Cover: Ron Gordon **Journey Through**
Web address: rgordon1.500px.com
Email address: rgordon@arach.net.au

Lien Botha www.lienbotha.co.za
p. 40 – **Yonder; Ditsong Museum of Natural History IV, Pretoria, 2011**
p. 64 – **Parrot Jungle; Maggie Laubser Street, Strand, 2009**
p. 88 – **Vergelegen, 2014**
p. 103 – **Parrot Jungle; South African Museum, Cape Town, 2009**
p. 126 – **Parrot Jungle; Loxodonta Africana, South African Museum,
          Cape Town, 2009**
p. 132 – **Untitled, 2014**
p. 144 – **Yonder; Bamako Senou International Airport II, Mali 2011**
p. 157 – **Yonder; Panari Hotel I, Nairobi, Kenya, 2011**

Jana van Niekerk pp. 24, 36, 119, 120, 137, 140
p. 68 – **Tor's Voyage (Because Of The Fish)**
p. 110 – Erich Staebe, photo provided by Jana van Niekerk
          (my great-grandfather)

pp. 10, 38, 52 – photos provided by Rosemund Handler
p. 28 – **Roots** by Natalie Railoun
p. 42 – Ben McAllen www.benmcallen.com
p. 72 – Uga Carlini
p. 74 – Kiana Lilly
pp. 84-85 – Anonymous
p. 87 – Jade Klara www.jadeklara.co.za
p. 106 – artist: yolowtfomg contact: yolowtfomg@gmail.com

The title of this collection is taken from Ted Hughes' poem, **For the Duration**:

As if you might still not manage to reach us
And carry us to safety.

Acknowledgements

The poets would like to acknowledge previous publication of a number of these poems (some in slightly different form) in the following publications:

Jana van Niekerk: **New Contrast, Botsotso, Kotaz, A Hudson View, Sentinel Literary Quarterly, Off-the-Wall Poetry 2012** and online at **Itch** and **Aerodrome**.

Rosemund Handler: **New Contrast, Carapace, New Coin, Botsotso, For Rhino in a Shrinking World** and various online poetry websites.

Natalie Railoun: **New Contrast** and **Botsotso**.

A note on the editorial process

Upon invitation by **Botsotso,** the poets co-edited this work and put the collection together themselves. This involved monthly meetings in a Cape Town coffee shop, at which they had the rare privilege of reading their poetry aloud to each other over cake. After a year of intense discussions, new friendships were made which survive to this day!

JvN: *For Thor Bovim*

RH: *In memory of AEJ*

NR: *In dedication to the journey
and its many travellers*

Contents

NAKED

൧ൠ

come to life!
over and outside
the small self

NR

❧ **Naked in the fields of Darling** ☙

We are naked in the fields of Darling

The way you jamb me up against the
headboard
there's nothing
like your face in my purple plums and
plum juice,
my sweet pig.

You're hotter than a bath.

I have a feint hard,
a knife wrapped in bandages,
you turn me inside-out like chokka.

This tight tomato like a pussy
my solid peach flesh flying,
a rock swims in the sea.

I look everywhere but your eyes,
your languorous thighs
You fine Fuckling,
Bint,
you are little more than your jewelbox
that my trinket finger opens.

Orchids and ferns and things.

It is dark and it is night.
I grew up at your body, working at
heights.

JvN

❧ Clifton Beach ☙

suntan cream and diesel
a chemistry
of bananas and drains

boulders boiling
steam rising from
skin and sandstone

a history of skin
a mythology of flesh
stored in every grain of sand

heart's blood
metres deep
thick with ageless lust

the murmurous tides of
countless generations
of burnished youth

yearning for itself
this cemetery of voyeurism
a vast assembly

of lecherous ghosts
peering between the spindly
legs of ogling old fuckers

shaky on the steps
soon to join their predecessors
for now free

of foolish inhibition
of stiff necks and stubborn joints
basking owl-eyed

stretching painfully
after a built bikini
silenced

by the biggest pair of tits
on the beach
then blurting

juicy with gestures
for the benefit
of cataracts and the hard of hearing

big tits have
neither eyes nor ears
for old fuckers

so what if salt water
drips like drool
from dropped jaws

and the sea is warmed
by incontinence?

RH

❧ Upside-down trees ☙

your hair has grown long
curled and tangled
from your dash
into the first summer rains
droplets collapse on my neck
pool around soggy kisses.
a cigarette comes to a careless end
in a half filled mug as you
draw my muddy feet to your chest
push me open into the earth
sinking

NR

❧☙

three new chairs
invite the stranger
you and I

NR

❧ Kunene ❧

Lush families of baobabs
drink their unruffled fill
swallows flit and feast on
dragonflies
as logs drift by in brown pools
where your voice is soft
and the unseen lurks
on crusts of sand

the mountains in thrall
to the soar and spin
the roar and weave
frothy precipices
burnished by the ringing sun
sadness and joy rising
as you plummet
vapour trembling in the haze
of your cold deep breath

RH

ᑖ Exhibition ᑣ

A figure dwarfed by an ancient landscape
physical and psychic wounds
reflected in the face of another
the shock of his body turning on him

the collision with mortality
carved in lines on his chest
a slow painful healing
a desperate urge to be as before

while becoming during and after breast cancer
awakened to suffering
to the grace and gift of each day
he is no more than a grain of sand

a will to survive

his life in ten shots

RH

❧ Sacred violent transition ☙

I love it at night,
the soft light.
Broken bees
and the bleating of my blue heart.

I live here for conversations about
names
and a breakfast future;
quick attention, great joyness in the
night set free.

my heart sang itself asleep

I hold it to myself,
this sacred violent transition in cold
water,
the warm deep underground sea:

Life is full of pancakes.
The sky is blue
and all of my pencils came through.

JvN

❧ What can I say about you? ☙

What I can say about you is this,
You
smile when I wake you
in the middle of the night
Sweetly Look dumbfounded,
wonder cheekily
if you are the butt of my jokes,
then lick me senseless.

What can I say when you

What I can say about you is.

What I can say about you is this,
there is no way
there is no going about this any other way,
I could not be another type
I mean,
nor are you.

What can I say.

What can I say about you but this.

It is that
you are so ferociously gentle I can't bear it,
you flay me lay me play me display me and
couldn't pay me.
I can't possibly you-know-what
without you
and when I do
it is just sad
not touching.

I am hopeless,
really lost,
it is very bad,
Dreadful.

I can't remember how I lived
without these parts of me
resting in your hand.

This is a love song
and I cannot sing

This is a life here
bitterly beautiful bring
your berry belly here

why I cannot say.

JvN

౪౬౩

dissimilar you
sentient and cognizant
can't play another

NR

ⅎ **Black bird** ⅓

When you said that word – it was the way you said it –
rage soared, spread its wings
covered me
a black bird with orange eyes
stabbing at muscle and bone
pecking at my veins
until they exploded in bloody flames
ripped through the sky
devoured indiscriminately.

Then fizzled.

Leaving the husk of what was between us
feathers stirring listlessly
waiting for an updraft
for that word to be unsaid
it was the way you did it
tossing it over your shoulder
like an afterthought
like a sack of garbage.
Twice.

Goodbye. Goodbye.

RH

ଛ Raising roots ଓ

wind thrashes and tears it up
wailing about ruin
we light up
the fire
a candle
to become a solitary
flickering opaque shadow

your pain erected into my sadness

bracing breeze
on softened limbs
makes the
surrender consoling
your enfolding warmer

rain drizzles on the berg
sweet honey after the blaze
our embers sleepier
seclusion deeper
insulation thicker

NR

❧ Property Developer ☙

A four-letter fanatic
expert in three languages
his deals caffeinated by curses
fuck's still his best
you like to fuck your wife
so what's wrong with fuck off

tippling testosterone
he pink-eyes the competition dead
slings snot pellets
at enemies and subcontractors
while grinding employees
between clashing implants

fuck buyers sellers
lawyers plumbers
fuck bankers most of all
the folded hands
of decision makers
sweat his haunted nights

hobble expletives
behind his bull neck
fuck gargling in his gullet
as hail-fellow-well-met
he belches gouts of godliness
when you least expect it

never takes the name
of the Lord in vain
never swears on the Sabbath
says karma is his favourite
five-letter word
don't fuck with it

RH

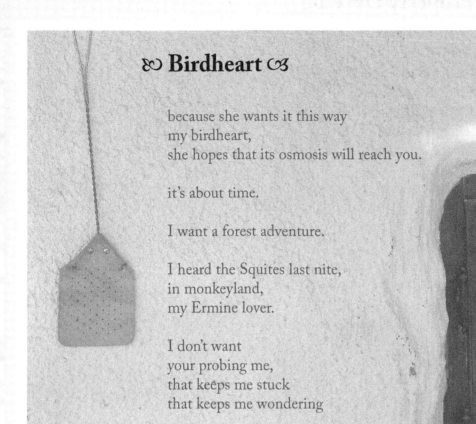

❧ Birdheart ☙

because she wants it this way
my birdheart,
she hopes that its osmosis will reach you.

it's about time.

I want a forest adventure.

I heard the Squites last nite,
in monkeyland,
my Ermine lover.

I don't want
your probing me,
that keeps me stuck
that keeps me wondering

JvN

What I like about getting older

is my friends are too
four or five, all in denial
    I've made an enemy or two
    for entertainment
irritation comes easy
I say fuckwit to the vexatious
    and become my least favourite insect
    a mosquito
sometimes a swarm of them
older mozzies bite deeper
    and don't give a damn
    if the flesh has a wrinkle or three
so long as it draws blood and tastes salty.
telling the truth
    leaves no time for making nice
    time is for wearing shabby clothes
that make even skinny people
look comfortable
    time is for avoiding wrinkle-loving mirrors
    or giving advice
or being touched
touch not being what it used to be
    I've stopped regretting
    stopped obsessing
forget to remember
trivial stuff
    like shopping lists
    and ego
and people who bore me
innocence of eye and ear
    long banished
    form and order an old habit
still dying hard
ambling from room to room
    unmindful
    pleasantly blank
the new disorder

RH

Full Moon on the Helderberg

a late afternoon sighs
through the hibiscus hedge
red headed petals nod while
we pinch at each other mockingly
aged into one vine
grown apart but knotted at the heart
traded fan dangled ideas for familiar hearth
old garden chairs
recalls of toddlers antics
damp eyed at the men emerged
almost over night in the door frames

years huge, pendulous
yield
bitter berries
sweet fruits
I don't think I have a memory before you
nothing considerable
nothing worth remembering

darkness clears the light
leaves the door open
to share a bed of fragrant evening blossom

we are who we have always been
we belong here

NR

❧ After rain ❧

After rain
we are in nature's room
of quiet noise
and you in your boy way
want to be busy.

You throw rocks
and call to surfers
and even yell about the sunset.

What are you doing, you say.
At that moment I am in fact
squeezing the fynbos to feel it.

Suddenly embarrassed, I say
Looking at the dewdrops on this bush.
It's so beautiful.

You come round and back to me
from the rocks
and bend your intensive little face
to the bush, to see.

I am dismantled by my love for you.
The spiderwebs, I say.

JvN

stranger to my skin
an alien seeking roots
quest of the soil-less

NR

❧ Himba man ☙

A figment
in the distance
a dervish of dust
cast out from the light
hewed from barren scrub
and a nobility of baobabs

heraldic on mountains
like herds of zebras
along trickling riverbeds
hoofed by proud Nguni
his calf and thigh spring
from a long ripple of wind

high scented
high-browed
his skull is sculpted
above features fine as feathers
and skin like a beetle's back
fluid as a shadow
he moves through the shadows
of his holy places

in his ears
along softly sandalled tracks
our tread is thunder
a platoon he sniffs from afar
he regards our sweat-pale faces
laden donkeys
bulging backpacks
with ancient stillness

as we fidget slightly
riveted by the intricate swirl
of bone and muscle
of dust and stone
in this land he roams
as a goat or a bird
weightless
almost free

RH

❧ Home/sic ❦

a smell out of nowhere
a jarring accent
in the penumbra
of a half life

asleep

a half-glimpsed beach
a sea of strangers
my name loud
on the sand

awake

I blink away the last decade
sleepwalking years
the view through the window
somebody's else

each day I'm somebody else

sifting through a library of selves
until I find one
that lasts an hour or a week
then flickers

blink

away a view I don't recognise
and cannot retain
a blur of tears
spilt in a language that has

already lost too many words

RH

Twin poems

I
Narrative Fiction

This cupboard was a gift.

My ornate late great grandmother's cupboard,
wanting French polish and reverie,
making my simple life seem wrong
when all it is, is artless.

If I put the cupboard on the beach and stop preserving it,
it will change.

I am a therapist who talks to the dead
and they can tell you my story
though you cannot hear.

I remember the first night I slept with you.

Words may not work for this.

He had slept with many women for pleasure
and now he was sleeping only with me.
He had, as he said, strong feelings for me.

The Greek hero who slept with women
and made no promises,
and they were slaves to him,
they didn't care that he fucked them and then left,
they lay in the sea, open,
howling at his departing sails
and hanging to have him
return.

This character,
is he just living in paradise
with his brain, his soul, and his barbarous libido,
a gigolo with an Achilles heel
and a poet who hates describing scenery?

I have no time to rush, he said,
nor to catch a flight

(not that there had been many such occasions,
it was an island after all.)

I am too busy driving the women wild
in the service of sex,
making grass huts
and writing this god-damn novel.

He felt like a man in a movie, only less attractive.
In reality he was every cliché in my book.

Peasant, poet, sailor, whore, the fleece and golden Minotaur.

He lay under the palm tree and remembered her.

Maria.

She was anxious around him.

Is it that you do not believe in love?

At the kitchen counter,
the old anger cut through me.
"I can't stand it," he said, and left.
How could there be,
it was no good.

Maria walked around with Pablo spilled in her blood.

Is there a place I can go?
What will make this better?
Something had caught him unawares
and would not let him go.

Spreading outwards and upwards towards him,
what had happened between them was
a fight to the death at the memory.

II
Writing

Oh my great sinking heart
it dreams and thinks itself
it reveals itself
it is terrified of being sense
of making heard,
known.

Outdoors there is no dust.
There is no locking it up
or keeping it for myself.

It is a paradise.

I make my own way.
I stand on your shore.
I listen to the demand of my heartstring.

Only the demand of my heartstring.

I remember the pause in it.

I play it.

When will you love me, Pablo?

JvN

ஓ Until first contact ௸

these days,
when everything tastes like poison
sleep comes in an uneasy veil
flood water suspends the body
hope is a denial
and no clasp in the cosmos for my coat.
too many words have lost their way
only sobs in foreign sounds
oil is scarce
salt has become rare
kindling a stone's throw away
and no spark to reach it

NR

ஓஇ௸

two years in my heart
I cut out your small footprint
gave it to your path

NR

⁊ If you read this... ⅋

What if you're inside me
your genes
a hollow clopping in my chest
a seeping of air like pus
in my lungs

your quick hard profile
taunts me from stray mirrors
a bitter line dismembers
the cat-o'-nine-tails
of my lips

a terrorist flickers in skin
whittles at bone
a slow tick-tock
from way back
a sudden torrent
of shameful whispers:

I will cut out my heart
bury it
you will dig it up
squeeze it
give it back
bloodless as dust

this whipping-post
of whispering
not even your death
will silence

RH

ITCH

Dog eat dog eat ----

Sir, your dog
my voice behind him
neutral but firm
man turns
I point to
the steaming pile
man grimaces
not my dog
sir I saw him do it
not my dog
you would recognise his shit
would you
my voice losing it
too big or too small is it
not yellow or brown enough
man flinches
I regret
the loss of tone
but man is steely
not my dog
his burnished Retriever
disagrees
won't go near the pile
but visits the mess
on the grass nearby
then lopes over
gives me a soulful grin
of apology
I call after
man's retreating back
wielding a plastic bag
I long to wrap
around his head
he's the gentleman
you're the dog
man turns
gives me the finger
so eat his shit bitch

RH

❧ Strictly between us ❦

It's the smell I miss
says D (divorcee)

sweaty shirts and fungal feet?
retorts M (survivor, twenty years)

the sweat's okay
if you work at it
says N (newly wed)

strictly between us
says D
sweat makes my scalp prickle

not the right spot
giggles N

so where do you prickle
asks D

never had a prickle
in my life admits N

new husband and no prickle?

gasps M

don't think so N replies

oh you'd know says M
I have my methods

like what asks D

a hunk on TV whispers M
Bert thinks I'm hot in bed

so you keep your eyes closed
says N

always M replies. Or it's Bert
and not a hope

I didn't need a hunk with Joe
rues D

but he did says N

men sighs M

RH

❧ What if ☙

This fish
slicker than the sea
still gasping
this somebody
who made pink birds
his skin no reason
to smell of strawberries
what if the mushrooms
maybe just the lilies
pushing through burnt woods.

JvN

❧ That's that ☙

Invisible is colder
says Josi, fifty, shivering
we should be bolder
stand shoulder to shoulder
but you can stare and not be stared at
glare and not be glared at
nobody cares says Penny, fifty-five
tear and not be torn adds Dina, fifty-two
what's that mean asks Josi
we can do hard gossip says Dina
what's that asks Penny
hard core gossip like tough love
they both hurt like mad
only one is good and one is bad
but nobody listens anyway says Kat, fifty-nine
we're invisible and that's that.

RH

꧁꧂

fancy bluebottles
precarious blue ribbons
time to head for shore!

NR

꧁ Blue Boy ꧂

He had been a jockey once, but now he was
a wanker. He meant, a banker. He smiled at
the receptionist. She seemed to be looking
down on him, in more ways than one. His
name was Aron but they had always called
him Little Boy Blue. He wondered if he had
a chance with her. She seemed to suggest
not. It was an Erectile Dysfunction clinic
after all. He sat down near the magazines. He
watched her from across the room, her little
plum breasts that pushed against the ledge as
she passed the clipboard. He got up, he went
over there and gave his form back in. She was
wearing a leather jacket. He smelt of sweat.
"All my life I've been fucking horses," he said.

JvN

&❦ Verbal parrot unattended ❦

This parrot is dead.
Or, at least, missing.
The parrot flew away
after the woman died of cancer.
She never would see a doctor.
Once, he nearly took her eye.

JvN

&❦

the feathered dancers
huddle on grim balcony
neon sign flashes

NR

❧ Age of Wisdom ❧

early morning, beachfront
-- I just don't want to wake up one morning
to find I'm forty or fifty and haven't --

all of twenty
youth not wasted on her
but life after fifty?

unthinkable –
even older?
at 74

hard up against the age of wisdom
Leonard Cohen
ditched religion

Paxil Prozac Ritalin
in favour of love
no cure for love

makes you wonder
why we squander

RH

❧ Ass-Man ❧

I am an Ass-Man, by Jana van Niekerk.

I like asses.

His, not hers.

I like your ass.

the way it follows you to the bathroom.

the way it cooks dinner.

it rises, it wants me to

slip it to you.

I get sad when I watch porn
o
because your ass is better than that,
it is meant for better things

basically

I want your ass
I want your ass
and it wouldn't be so bad
assed
if I got lucky once in a while
it would smile.

JvN

❧ Jy tel my toe op ☙

Jy kom tel my toe op
in jou groot skip
met gange
en kamers wat ruik soos my ou dae

en jy's die kaptein
in jou pers polka-dot hemp,
die appels van 'n verlate kus se boord
lê sap in jou mond
en jy kyk my half skurf aan
en ruik soos my maat.

Al golwend ry ons daai see.

Jy anker haar
met jou swart skoen
en jou hand
op die skouer van haar wiel.

Ons eet vis
en ek is bewus
van alles
en niks,

blindelings

staan ek op die skemerdek
en dink aan die aand wat voor my lê,
daar oor die baai
so mooi,
so pienk.

JvN

ᘒ Spaarsleutel 235880 ᘓ

Na my kindernagte,
deur lakens ingekerker,
en na my malseisoen
kom ek tot op die punt, nou
waar ek my voordeur probeer oopsluit
met spaarsleutel 235880
(soos jy dit geskryf het).
Een, twee, drie keer
probeer ek dit in die donker
welwetende,
dis fout
maar die digte vassit
die nie-wil-draai-nie
die ding in my hand
is oombliklik al
wat ek van jou besit.

JvN

൦ல

the break is right now
this moment I am broken
one step at a time

൦ல

shutting down the blinds
slowly descending into
my aching body

NR

❧ Sleep ☙

Stippled with light
my grown son
splayed like some inert
sun-drenched amphibian
in a disorder of
limbs and linen
clutches at sleep
with clenched fists
squeezes from it
oblivion like a love affair
without peaks or plateaus

leprechaun memory
tousles his hair
freckles his nose
flashes the grin
of a small boy
turned fugitive from
outsize dreams

RH

❧ A memory of Leah ☙

Hot sun on my back
Leah at the front door
fitted skirt and stilettos

midnight hair in rollers
arms folded tight at sight of me
the fearsome raider of restful
cupboards
fragrant with chocolate

Leah sniffs
the wind of her disapproval
wafts past me

RH

SINS

CBEO

you are happiest
effortlessly cutting fish
your forefathers' knives

NR

&o Black ca

He is resting
against the morning
heavy hide
cradled by blonde grass
he is enthroned
to the end of time

eyes will behold him
enshrine him
in memory and illusion
his outline fading as the light
grows harsher
and the morning trembles
to afternoon

his slow eye sidles
until a horn-shaped moon
tattoes it with dollar signs
his half-sleep no
anaesthetic
for the famished vigil
the grasses already
leaking and foetid

the violent dawn
drenches the sky
in scarlet obscenity
they have eaten
their own faces

RH

❧ Sister ☙

You were like an egg
unbroken
smooth and round
till you cracked
spilt all over the place

dripping
you implored
save me sister
but I was buried to the neck
the truth is

you wanted me beneath you
to stand on my bones
shatter them like eggshell
use the splinters
to put out my eyes

RH

❧ Pasia ☙

was the name
of my Russian grandmother
Pasia Krusavitskaya
Ochi Chorniya
dark eyes

in Judith's Paarl
she was Pauline Davidoff
each day in Africa
she gazed dreamily
up at the Tsar's palace

the family home
on a rise close by
warm with company
governesses servants
eager suitors

never less than four
the smoke of good cigars
spicing the harsh music
of Russian French German
Pasia's hostile gaze

turned-down mouth
disapproved of Africa
of listless highveld air
heat and thunder
of noisy grandchildren

who beat her at cards
she turned her back on us
you humbugged me
sulked for a while
played Patience

her cinnamon bulkes
scenting the neighbourhood
hot chips scalding joy
the reek of blackened chicken
distressed even the birds

she fried fish
that smelt of drains
and brought her to despair
only in Moskva
did the fish taste of butter

the butter of snow and sunlight
the sunlight of spring

she hummed nagged
gave orders
her squat shadow
looming over John
the Zulu servant

his warrior ancestry
misspent on his knees
polishing the stoep
she had favourite daughters
grandchildren

disfavour
like dishonour
disabled
until a poppy seed bun
made amends

a proud sad bad painting
scribbled mouth
burnished cheekbones
black eyes blued with grease
she tottered on stilettos

stockings a whirring of insect wings
buns on the insides of her knees
moods the colour of her hair
peevish pink to arrogant purple
bombarded us with –

Aristocrut!
You are from Aristocrut
but you behafe like dogs!
we chased Zulu
the terrified terrier

bribed granny for sweets
in exchange for an audience
tsarina of her world
Africa an interlude
she turned her nose up to

ghosts of Russia
startled in corners
strange hats pulled faces
from the shadows
old boxes staring portraits

ancient perfume
bedded down with mothballs
as she snored and thrashed
at the dingy light
we giggled

applied smears of lipstick
eye shadow
dangled long earrings
strutted in high heels
bulging from bunions

the white gauze of a hat
like falling snow
in the mirror
once we found
her weeping

over flimsy faded
letters in Russian
she said they wrote of fear
flight in darkness
the pain of snow blindness

at seventeen
in a high-ceilinged room
she married a pressing suitor
with a silken tongue
when they fled Moskva

she was bloated with anguish and child
enduring for one love
while losing another
in heat that chilled her
she dressed in black

past present future
a single country
the long widowhood
of a love so fierce
that Africa was humbled

Mademoiselle Krusavitskaya

RH

❧ Sister Insurrection ☙
(for Khadija)

this kind of honesty will always be
loose, sharp, quick, tart
spat from the aching mouth
of a custodian who will
spread out naked and angry for it
hemorrhaging raw word
sacrificing blood –
in the hope you will be
pulled up to her scope
ruffled enough to see
the coarse, old ache
a truth that cannot be filed down
to a square manicure or
refined to a neat curl
sucked back under an aromatic tongue

NR

♥ What about mothers ♥

What about mothers who fuck their daughters,
what about them?

Well what about those motherfuckers.

No matter:
No mother.

What about motherfuckers who marry their mothers.
(Why bother)

What about fucking mothers that matter,
that marry,
then motherfuck their daughters,
like mine.

Well, what about that?

What about getting off of me.

What about getting off on me?

What about getting
your hands off
of me
and keeping your eyes on the road?

But no matter
how much I scream
she does not.

And I have to keep the car on the road.

No matter.
Keep on me. Keep on me.
You know you can.

JvN

❧ The Russian Room ☙

The electric heater burns my shins
as you knit peacefully
yarns creeping close to the fire

and the Russian vases
sharp blues and reds
softened with age

yet resilient in the marbled light
Limoges and Royal Albert miniatures
coy behind glass and wood

you the amulet, the extra rib
I cradle in my chest
to disempower the bruising years

your burnished head
fine this hour
above concentration so pure

I am free to gaze for minutes
wondering if I can touch you
at last

RH

❧ Another country ☙

Reaching for the wine
you accidentally
brush her breast
she doesn't flinch

your wife beside you
bares her teeth
lipstick on the glass
the moon stops

at another woman's ear
crafts a silvery shell behind
a scarlet drop of earring
you crush the glass

wine on the table
blood on your hand
her nails score numbers
into your palm

she reads your map
knows her way
across the porous borders
of your country

tracks blood spoor
across your skin

RH

❧ Second sex ☙

You closed the bedroom door
asleep on me
just as she had done
so many years before.

You both wanted something from me.

She, to be my bedmate –
she told me with fists,
the walls painted blue,
and satin sheets on.

You look with eyes that see me.

You, to be my playmate
used her finger to make me come,
taking in what I wear or do,
she thought I might be
you drink me with your eyes,
your mother
confess, years later,
what your favourite line was in a
poem I wrote you
and are so full of regrets
my dear.

JvN

❧ Zettie ☙

you are lilac
swaying gently
scotch mist in open fields of off white

purple velvet, you become heavy
your laughter crackles, bubbles
about
imitation flowers in half filled plastic
bottles
bobbing on the mound of a
winter sun burial with
modest wooden headpiece

for a moment
I am fearful you are cold and alone
I am cold, I am alone
rain spots the sand
tears spot my blouse
we walk away
we drive away

you are lilac lace swaying
drizzle a monkey's wedding
remember always your
purple velvet Sunday hat with feathers

last night you were happy in my dreams

NR

orange clivia
out of half moon moss shadow
secret burning sun

NR

❧ Crazy Monkey* ❧

The day that takes you forward.
It's ebbed away from me like so much sea.
I say hello to the trees and the trees say an aeroplane back to me.

Goodbye, water.
I am hopeful, hurting.
This thing moves through me like a rake.
Skin, hair, blood, cold shell.
They tore that baby shred to shred.

Darling God,
I heard the magic owl
in Coca-Cola waves.

Listen to the lights,
you say.
This is your day.
A warm skin on my back.

The trees are going ahead of us.
The moon like firelight.
Time is travelling so fast.

I say a prayer to the wind
and the grasses say a whisper back to me.

They had dew on their lip.
They all failed.

Eden, what kind of a name is that?
We were just beginning to negotiate.

The birds played their song.
This thing rakes through me.
I move right through it.
It moves right through me like a rake.

JvN

---

* Brett Goldin, a young actor killed alongside his friend
in an execution-style murder in Cape Town in 2006.

❧ Do I need to hold my breath to receive you? ☙

How did Adam and Eve live in the garden? Chiefly, without worry.
They were in communion with bliss. (This is good for me.)
They used their senses. They followed their impulses.
God took care of tomorrow (if they knew what that is).
There is the Khoi, swimming in the Southeaster.
We are all fallen angels.

What did they say? They said don't eat this apple.
The apple is the smear of earthy shame.
The wind is blowing. Mamma's eating chocolate biscuits.
Because I am rebellious. Because it takes humility to receive.
Because I wanted to see more.

JvN

ೞ

a moth stops struggling
spider waits for me to leave
to inspect her meal

NR

PLAY

ᛞ Men on boats ᛒ

talk a lot about fucking women
also other men
fists, doorknobs, holes in walls
and the usual body parts

a sailor says I fucked a boy
moffiearselicker
better to fuck a goat
hey you gotta try

before you die
siesjong no lips just a gat
a lips man, are you?
Professor MajoraMinora

men on boats
grown flabby and farty
until the bite of the sea
gets worse than its bark

and dawn brushed pink
by God's finger
traps light lancing through mist
striking gold

in a dance of dolphins
on an ocean like glass
by 8 am
they're back to fucking

RH

❧ For Elaine ☙

Nobody's had a life like mine
a war of beatings incest crime
my parents drank the trailer stank
of brandy beer cheap wine

my father was the first:
virginity, sweetie, is the worst
you'll be ready when you wed
you'll thank me one day he said

then his friends all six
got up to their tricks
all six on the unmade bed
until the sheets ran RedRedRed

pregnant at thirteen
my father lean and mean
took me unawares
pushed me down the stairs

as rain fell like blood
the child was born in mud
I held her as she cried
then turned blue and died

met a man who fell in love
called me his pretty turtledove
pulled a knife on our wedding night
because the sheets stayed WhiteWhiteWhite

spat at me kicked me said I was a whore
threw me bodily out the door
pregnant again for my sins
this time I pushed out healthy twins

still fell for guys
who told me lies
being dyslexic
made me unwise

turpentine on the toilet cover
the twins inhaled it was my lover
got so bad they couldn't breathe
he bought me a funeral wreath

lucky Jesus dope and booze
showed me the way to beat the blues
thank Christ for brandy beer cheap wine
nobody's had a life like mine

RH

❧ Little boy, my baby1 ❧

I'm only a little helpless baby
if the wolves must eat me
they must eat me.

I hold on to you a bit
you are also alone

you wake up shouting and farting
I have to hold you while you poo
you're only the second man whose underwear I've sniffed
you can spend an hour alone looking at the wall
I need to be in the same room as you
you are heavy when you sleep
you snuffle like a piggie
I want you to maul me

like old times, except for the small red cut above my

little boy

in my bed full of wee
even a splash of blood
yeasty poo and curdsy breast-milk
fresh-baked semen
the smell on my fingers
marmite
salty marine
my pork lunch

my perfect child.

already you know
crying
the pain of hunger gas wetness a needle
already there is dirt under your fingernails

I thought you
portaled here through me
but look you are the gateway

I smell like a zoo
I love you so much in your sour jersey
I empty this breast into you like a machine-gun

JvN

73

꧁꧂

year of wooden horse
wildish, unafraid and sure
courage galloping

NR

❧ Mother ☙

In my element
no longer my element
motherhood relinquished
light as a leaf

I am found again
once found
confined
like a spider with grains of spiderlings

engraved on her back

like once found wings
and flew
then lost them
I am confused

by chains

long after
I dreamed in secret
that I'd skipped
an absconder

the one that thought she'd got away

RH

❧ The birthday present ❧

All night these flowers have been drinking,
I was born at 3.32

All day my thoughts were thinking,
only of you.

Where is the party
and why am I not there?

How can they take you
away from our safe lair?

I am white and pure and strong,
the Greatest Polar Bear.

But someone else has Got you
and left me in the air.

All night these flowers were drinking,
all day I thought of you.

I held you in my heart
and let you see me through.

I cup you in my hand,
I see you in my eyes.
Your spirit shining truer
than any Birthday Prize.

My love for you is sparkling.
The sight of you, Divine.

I know by silken bonds
I cannot call you mine.

I bring you what I can,
I give you all my cake.
I kiss your cheek at night
and hear you when you wake.

Where is your birthday present,
your joy to be alive?

Your moment is the now one
and i'll wait till you arrive.

JvN

ೞ

elegant pale feet
dancing ripe glossy cherries
smooching the lush grass

NR

❧ Something for the little boy ☙
(caught in a custardy battle)

Some Thing lies
in the pocket of potatoes, shifty, shifty.

Petrified Something.
I could throw it out
(quickly).

Perhaps I would still see Something
If Something is there.

Something on ice.

Something with fur.
Something with rice.

I don't want to
touch Something
or feel Something
that's not mice.

JvN

❧ 18 Months ☙

How did it happen
that you became a small person
with your own scars

from beginning in the hospital
listening to the rain
with only your eyes?

your weight on me almost like emotion

Once I had no baby, now you're as tall
as the neighbour's child

she's combing your hair and telling you
the story of what's happened

even though you only burble and point –
let's find shelter
it's starting to rain.

JvN

❦ The pick-up-poo lady ❧

Her dog on a lead
she picks up his poo
looks about her
picks your dog's up too

the job is thankless
poos unending
the poo lady undaunted
is forever bending

saint or fool
I think she's pretty cool

RH

❧ Has Been ☙

Once upon a time when I was a little girl I was much littler than I am now. I was the size of a bean I was really teensy tiny they kept losing me. My mum would get in a tizz: "Where have you BEEN, Bean?" she would ask when I turned up. I was a sugar bean. I was round and plump like a jumping bean. A jelly bean. I was a has bean. The dog licked his chops and grinned. My mum bought a leash. My father came home. "I've had ENUFF of all this mash," he said and tried to slam the swing door. My mum tucked me under her armpit. All night the dog licked me with his twister tongue and all night the lights from my father's car criss-crossed the room, criss-crossed the room, criss-crossed the room.

JvN

❧ Melkbaai ❧

hydraulic wrecking balls and steely animals
devour mortared records
bite by bite the musty voorkamers digested to outyd
outstanding housing postulates
perfect arcs and angles
glinting marble tiles and glass
cosmopolitan blueprints open to no favorites only sound
finances

tip toe over the blinking robots now at every intersection
tip toe over a slice of crumbling boundary
into the soft sand
where everybody can now make –
an angel
a castle
a dance
an eager appearance before the ocean
splashing in bathing suits, petticoats
in onderbroek

NR

ೞ

pressure and effort
ignore a sunrise invite
spine to the skylight

NR

❧ Happy poem ☙

racing from my cheery heart
you are
definite
liquid
saturating the page
even before the ink
releasing your seed
as if you know
how quickly this mood
may evaporate

NR

❧ Gem in the garden ☙
(A children's story)

Mommy!
Come find me.

I am looking for you.
I am looking for you in cupboards
and traces,
their faces
and all the old places.

I am looking for you in the Aquarium.
I am looking for you in my Cell phone.
I am looking for you in the man with
the Djembe drums.

I am hoping to see you.

Why do birds hop?
Why do heads ache?

There is a garden each to each
where I am put,
where I hide things.

I will come back for you, you said.

Mommy, come find me!

I am felt by the Fall,
I am chilled by the sun.

The wind shocks me!
The sea bites me!

I never wanted to be lonely like this.

Love lines my belly
like a pitted peach jelly.

I am looking for you everywhere:

Ruby shoes.
Reading winds.

I am in my garden, every day.

And the garden whispers to Gem:
you bear sad things
by holding them.

JvN

a-float in your cove
ancient salts removing scale
weightless in your womb

NR

MARROW

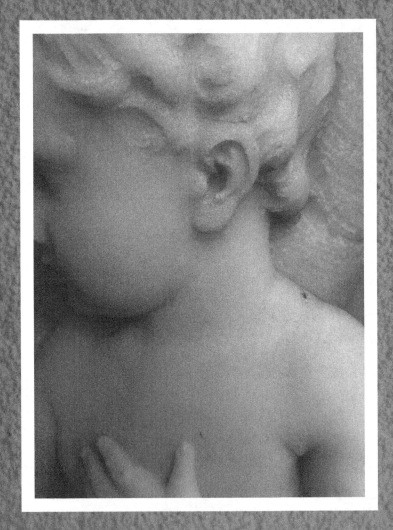

ೞ

cooking in silence
a woman's meditation
some salt for her pot

NR

❧ House ❧

There are many mansions.

Cool in summer, very very warm in winter:
People who build their own houses care.

Bang bang bang goes the house.
The house is speaking.
Two birds attack each other amorously and look at me.
We find a quiet place to copulate
in our shelter.

The house says
you were here
I eat your vegetables.
My dog watches me.
Flap flap flap
the wind in plastic
the eaves
the wood groans
squeaks
sighs
says it's all lies.

JvN

❦ Before she met you ❧

she thought herself fruity
subtle yet tangy
not quite ripe
sweet-sour at the pip

a pale apricot
or a mango with strings
even a lemon
scouring the palate inside out

the day you saw her
pungent earthy stains
clamoured from her fingers
would not be expunged

your nostrils flared
she was an onion
biting between your teeth
crackling on your cringing
tongue

you stayed the course
pared to the heart of her
that takes a man
now that takes a real man

RH

❧ Wife ☙

The floor shakes
it's her heart
fallen through it
splintering the panels
at sight of him
his eyes shooting blood
she hears the children
stirring in their beds
backs towards them
making herself as wide
as the room
as barbed as safety wire

but he can smell her
she's transfixed
as he licks her
from his lips and shows
her the weapon
that he's always used
that gave her two children
only this time the bullet
is not for her
it's the baby first
she begs for his life
howls for God and mercy

as he heaves her across the room
after the shot
there is quiet
enough time for hope
to throw herself across the girl
delicate bones moving like ants
against her mother's chest

at the back of her neck
she feels his hand hot
not even sweaty
steady for a moment
as if something might change
then her head snaps back
the shot bursts her eardrums
she no longer hears whimpers

sees his face flattened by hate
dry like a riverbed
without the rain of tears
sees shapes in the darkness
before it falls on her

RH

ஐ The Hum-drum ☙

We open a magic golden box,
the whole pad of me is feeling.

What's in there?
This idyll.
A wind-up dog.
Five kids after football.
Only a bead.

JvN

& Loss ⊂ঽ

Her pores full of sand
her irises leached of
river brown tears
she has waited
for time to pass
but it hasn't bothered to
she finds
there is little to say
about time
and all that healing

their lives were joined shadows
even his absence present
if the day cowed her
he'd pick up her heart
between gentle palms
put it in his shirt
two budgies she
never dreamed
would fly apart

they fed each other ideas
delicate teaspoons
so as not to choke
on them
sometimes she rages
blames the silence
mostly she repudiates it
with those he has loved
Prokofiev
Bruce Springsteen
Joan Baez

she puzzles
how to contain him
bottle the gentle buzz in her ear
keep the tiny bowls
in which he gathered her tears
sipping together
laughing a little until
the sticky dawn took him
and she buried her face

in the dent of his pillow
the dent remains
made by her fist
his scent long gone
she vows to dig him up
drape herself
in his funeral shroud
wear his collarbone
as a necklace
his fingernails
as keepsakes

but she can't barter
with boneless ashes
not even a tooth
to conceal
beneath her tongue
now his voice
in her head
has abandoned her
all that is left is
the key in the door

her head tilted for it
every afternoon
at five o'clock

RH

ℰ Domestic Bliss ℰ

Goodness knows what happened to my
last e-mail.
I keep a little diary of days,
is someone's heart beaten between us?
Because something stronger than my
love for you
is twisting in your guts.

The yello dog looked at me with its
bright yello face:
"There must be some secret for my life."

You are beautiful,
but you are burnt.

Oh Canary with teeth,
you Manduca Hawk Moth –
edgy, a thick cage, you can't touch it.

There must be some code.

And you forget how lovely you thought
this once was,
and how open.
One bowl and one cup, and here we are.
I fed you in my body
when everyone else was gone.

See me run.

The beginnings of soup,
"Enquire first floor."
Rice pudding. Tuna rice
(and all that stuff about aubergines.)

I have lots of little crevices to fill.
I touch you so that you don't, and I will.
So that you know they exist,
so you know they are yours.

That food came to sit in you like
certainty.
The descendants of your rhubarb –
the dynamics of disgust,
whatever notion of failure or blindness
you might have had.

It took courage in parking lots.

I think I'll just have a little bath,
creating more problems in the laundry-
line.
Garment care, Tuesday to Friday, the
comfort of awfulness,
the way pain begins to separate us.

Some soft house slippers and intimations
of intimacy

– for whatever reason.
You have no clue.
Your letters shouting on the fridge:
"Who knows if you are a Beastie, but you!"

"You have a kind of domestic wrath, darling."
Cutting off the parts of you that hurt me.
Whisky amidst the cleaning products,
and an angry wank
is no good.

Allah came to me in the pudding;
he said
it's perfect
even and although it's burnt.

I've raised you with supposition,
I've raised you with prayers.
I bit you in Paradise,
I apologise.
For whatever reason.
I have no clue.

Perhaps I need to temper my joy,
watching your washing drying.

How is it for us
doing a violence to yourself,
even just the way you talk about me
in poems like this.

Something in me is abhorred by
something in you.

JvN

C3 80

silence an answer
conjurer, agitator
echoing the truth

C3 80

woman held ransom
by his green root of evil
she trades gold lotus

NR

ℰ The living ℭ

dimmed passage light
fuck buddy on speed dial
uncle Jack distilled on ice
sublingual medication on standby
self empowerment shoved in the
draw

no
blanket
no
cushion

unstable weather
shakes the wooden frame
rustles up a cautionary groan
cold, red eyed tosses and turns
tweak the pinions

gathering clouds disconnect
for the transfer to rip
across the sheets
ultraviolet

NR

❧ Translux Love: A journey to the end ❦

"This is why we're here?" she said.
"This hill, as good as any
what can we do but look,
this view from the top –
all this beauty."

Him: caught in a dead man's memory
crunching thoughts like stones
frozen flyboys
Translux love
shaven lubes
slippery with frogs
he remembers her slappable tush.

Virgin boy
virgin boy
she thinks
I don't like the word pageant:
lives captured
like these stones
in a dead man's eye.

Are you hearing my message?
she asks, or would like to ask
Vodacom
in sumptuous crunchy thoughts like stone
slippery with frogs
in a dead man's throat.

His idea of making love:
wading through the annals.
"Napier" the sliding said
again, slippery frogs
she considers
the wait of the place,
his slappable face.

– so she stops to whistle, or toot
the smell of Acacias, Mimosa
the value
of slipping, sliding and hiding
lying in weight.

They've arrived:
Absolute Elsewhere,
a frog's eye view.
You should have married a nice guy
he said
and taken the optional egg.

JvN

ꙮ 'n Gedig aan ons ongebore seun ꙮ

O maar jy's 'n slim kind en 'n mooi
jou kop is sterk,
jou gevel skeer rooi.

Jy loop die aarde ongewond
maar jou pa se trek is om jou se mond.

Ek soen jou gesig wat ons twee was,
al ons lyf en leed is in jou ingepas.

Kyk, jou trane rol uit my oog
en jou woorde is geskiet uit jou pa se boog.

Ek lief julle twee van die selfde:
ek lief jou, en in jou, my helfde.

JvN

ꙮ

sour sweat bedding of
dank misery asylum
dark dog still barking

NR

❦ Cellular memory ❧

woman be strong
station still so far for
resigned tender outstretched arms

pushing on past promising billboards
rubbished by black and blue knowledge
that has become your survival
in this city

promising billboards
torn from their loftiness
glamour shredded to shit
by what is needed to do
for
safety
food
5 bob chips
A bar of lux(ury)
5 rand airtime vouchers
Taxi fare
keeping up with another's shoes

push on with memorized lullaby
placing the distance for you
soothing what is harsh

woman with heavy candy striped canvas bag
move on with
every blistered imprint
your longing for
the Eastern Cape
your grandmother
the baby girl you sent home last May

NR

CS♾️ЄⱭ

bean pods turning beige
the pumpkin's skin still too soft
turnips are sprouting

CS♾️ЄⱭ

cool early rise with
morning's name slightly darker
coffee brewed stronger

NR

❧ Things we found in the flood ☙

(Faure – Winter 2013)

flood after flood
unearthing
more than
weathered legs of fixtures
pudding bowls with fissures
fused fittings
loose footings
putrefying remains

in the driveway
debris droops, sprawls and stinks
drained and filthy –
the septic tank flushed out
sun dries and sanitizes

a long grubby sorting begins
heavy, malodorous and bitter
battered owner's handbook/ deed of sale
a car/house once owned/ owned us

poignantly we rescue
forgotten baby photos
the hat I wore when we married
a Lego bionicle 10 years old
a Teddy Pendergrass and Bob Marley album
have all survived
joy
one love
for being
washed out
washed into
the backstroke of a deeper reality

NR

❧ Almost ☙

Against the window the air
surges liquid
trees groan
leaves tumble

in a sudden flare
of anguished light
a trickle on the roof tiles
silence for an instant

I wait. Open the door
face the vanishing storm
night sounds intrude
the cicadas loud

branches stirring and settling
scratching the dirt
I close the door
lean against it

the day's heat thick
with the scent of something aborted

RH

❧ Moments from the brim ☙

the rubber tree
a body of water
my tea, cold after an hour

sun city's chimneys push plumes of smoke
all day, all night people are cooking, boiling
whatever it is
unemployment and short time can dish up

a siren cuts through serious thought
yellow and gray songololo
rattles its graffiti and travels through the
landscape
splitting it;
water color blue with white cloud and
hadida
goats exiting a field, tails whipping the
wind

yellow marble eyes move closer
I push a few apples through the fence
into their endless masticating

NR

FREEFALL

౫౩౪౬

narcissism flaps
arrogant wings rise, sun waits
incineration

NR

❧ The bridge ☙

Fractured icicles of light
a blind necklace
suspended from

the hard heart
of the city
he climbs jewel by jewel

until he reaches the
highest point
where its fire

is defeated by stars
the night spins with them
with promises of change

but the moon is threadbare
he's not fooled
not any more

he catches the light
between his teeth
stills the tremor

of his right hand
easy now
below him the water

jaws wide
glistens oily
black as the back of a hippo

he thinks
you'll never see one of those again
then jumps

RH

ೞ

lonely pine composed
dropping miniature arrows
in the heart of spring

ೞ

hollowed out belly
unfamiliar hunger
angst's corset too tight

NR

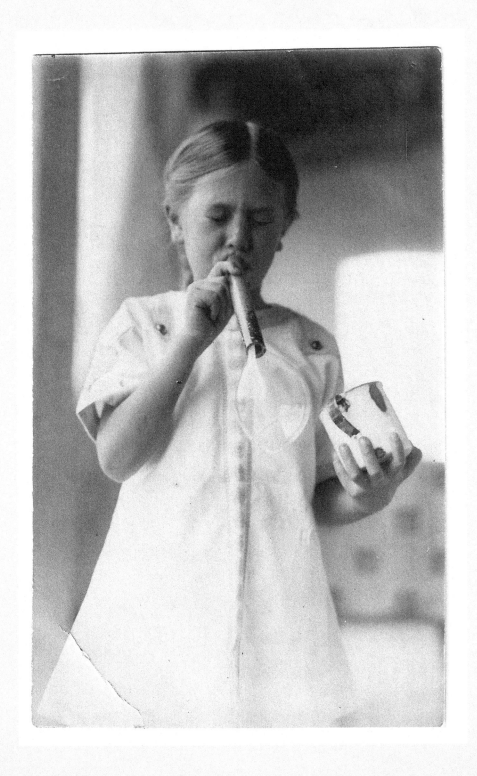

✵ Jump!* ✵

Here I still am in the hot and dusty air,
no jump could ever release me.

I am still earthbound
still opening my eyes to the doors
still seeing in mortal worlds
stars
and your sun still
threatens to circumvent me.

Not stepping backwards
tearing ice
nor bubbling on the shore.

They sent a man to fetch
me, to say:
We have the helium and we're here.

JvN

---

* Felix Baumgartner became the world's first supersonic
skydiver in 2012, freefalling from outer space.

❧ Jellyfish: for William Blake ❧

O jellyfish
thou art sick
the invisible tides
that seethe
in the night
in the howling void
have found out
thy bed of midnight blue
and with brute satanic glee
have cast you from the sea

RH

❧ Fence-sitting ☙

Mecca will always murmur
your name alone
you reply in sorrowful supplication
finding your answers in
hushed prayers and a prophet's wisdom

I discover pieces of myself everywhere
in shooting stars and
coffee colored rock pools

the wilderness calls out an oasis
prophet's hand reaches for more soul
rock pools shimmer my calling

here we are fixed on a rail
leaning
we clutch to
convictions of love
to the fear that

our seats may be taken

NR

ಐ Breakdown of a musician ೞ

There are times she tells herself
 one day she'll play out
the hours and days
     of electricity and blackouts
     her switched-on switched-off brain
plundering eyeballs
scribbling itself on the ceiling
on piano keys
     illegible coils of repetition
     that resonate like a solution
treachery she can't pin down
can't fight back
she doesn't climb walls
     she thinks about cancer
     about metastases in treble clefs
about dying just to feel alive again
they won't give her more pills
a sip of water
          dry swallow
          the sleeping draught wakes her
long before the small hours
when shadows have claws
and corners glare
          her skin will stretch no further
          she calls for her mother
the broken sound floats
a note she remembers
raising a slow finger to touch
     before it fades

RH

❧ Disquiet Poem ☙

I have become a woman who lives in a big house,
alone.

I am just momentarily busy
and don't open the possibility of regret.

Fame for sentiments,
I write because I am angry and I cannot love.

And this obsessiveness doesn't help me,
all the books I read at once.

I am one of those women now,
whom I have always wanted to be.

My aspiration
to warm my bones in the sun.

I will know
that I was a person here once too

when Death, which comes to do my giving over
for me

sings,

"Ash rain, salad rain,
loss is loss,
my darling."

JvN

❧ Suicide gene ☙

Mist gathers
a black hole lurks
somewhere close by
boulders crowd in

generations back
uncles brothers cousins
unleashed an atavistic thread
that unspooled in blood

gun water rope
a building high as hope
a train like a beckoning finger
seconds that never end

I see the same face
over and over and over
the indelible imprint
of what has been
what is
what must be
if those images
of you
are me

RH

❧ Death ☙

I cannot do death with my head
too hard to do this
just as I cannot do birth
this is it
I am afraid I will be left desolate
by this life
death of what, the body dying
perhaps I won't be alone
looking in your eyes,
distracted
I may even wait impatiently,
I might miss it.

When I turn
I see only the pink golden
peace where my life was,
this goes on and on
and walking in the shadow green
dark
now know this is
so much fear
only another way.

JvN

❦ Fever ❧

Light scratches my lids
the moon leers
fine and sharp
as a splinter of bone

night creatures loom
over the trembling bed
the crunch of a branch
hangnails across glass

I flinch
cry out

somebody brings water

RH

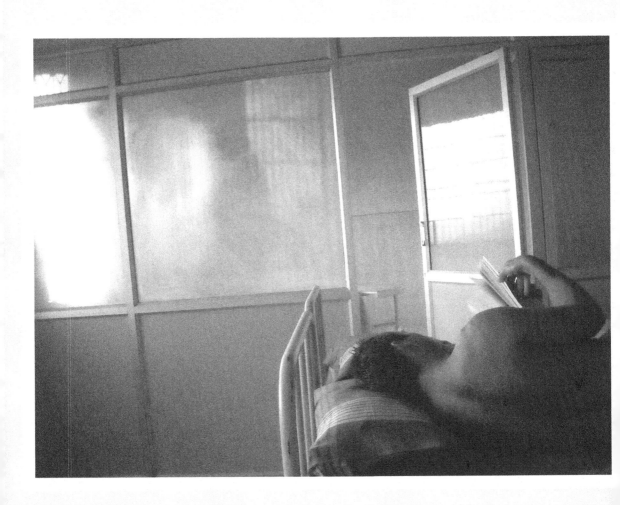

❧ Grief work joy ☙

Grief work
is a story
about dead relationships
and different kinds of loss –
Mr Henderson, via his diagnosis.

And then I saw him run across the sky.

My husband could not sleep
on his orange carpet and the red futon,
unless it was dark
by mid-afternoon.

Something had seized hold in childhood
and would not let him go.

I think I strode in,
progressive, paralysed
desperate or perhaps just ready,
when your therapist does all the talking.

At this time
I was an intern clinical psychologist
at the local general hospital

not a medical person,
my first wedding anniversary
(or maybe not)
I can't remember
now.

And it rendered him
at the age of thirty

dying.

Aggrieved

he said he was.

I suffered more than he.

A virgin,

dying.

He suffered more than me.

JvN

❧ Mabandla ☙

I put you in a poem
so I won't forget you
Ma-ban-dla

I heard about a woman
who set herself alight
Ma-ban-dla

madness or despair
you turned away
as if you didn't care

as if burning flesh
does not sear your nostrils
Ma-ban-dla

old young man
one leg missing
more present

in the pinned-up pant
with dirt in the creases
Ma-ban-dla

three more months
says the social worker
in 2006

your child's chest
rising falling
how long must your ribcage

pierce your flesh
before somebody notices
that your stick lies in the dust

and the door
of your shack
is opened by a stranger

RH

122

∞ Without warning ∞

In the chill dark
after midnight
warm against her back
he died

his stillness pawing at her sleep
as always she murmurs his name
a trickle of saliva on the pillow
the sheets cooling

without his stuttering breath
her eyes snap open
she turns
touches his cheek

feels icy stubble
and rage
that he has gone
without her

RH

∞ A night at the theatre ∞

excited butterflies
trace and titillate
the eyes
seeing
the rabbit is alive, plucked from the hat

so bold we are
suspended precariously
above gravity
only seconds before we become undone

to believe
that the star spangled sword
which will halve us
will also assemble our severance

conjure! summon!
juggle the smoke and mirrors

gasp
grasp at the chimera

until

the coppery penny falls from
behind our ear
followed by the crisp flipping of
cards cascading to wherever they will

NR

❧ Dream-catcher ☙

first evenings of March are sublime
even with the heat
hot wind flutters the drapes
jingles the chimes

a cool bath
your hands on my belly
anticipating
another kick
another little fist
willing to hold this sweetness in our hands
rub his cheeks against ours
hold him close to our sated hearts

we rub my stomach like a giant genie's lamp
check the hospital overnight bag once again, just in case

at night
we lay spooned and pillow propped
under the billowing lace breeze
heavily expectant

NR

❧ Saved ☙

sunrise and sunset emerge the same
from the mouth of the shadow spectre

reality could be a hallucination
or worse
a lie

*

naked in free fall
swindled, out of sparkles

but all light is one light
any warmth a savior
every hand is gracious
every breath grateful

to the clouds in free verse
to the creature in free form

NR

ELEPHANT

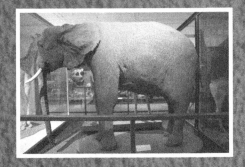

❦ Boomslang ❧
(for DH Lawrence)

A snake came to my hiking path
On a hot hot day
And I cowering from the sun
He unspooled
Lay brown-silk-scaled
Across scalding stones for a moment
Then threaded up a fire-dead bush
Peered
Hooded slightly
So honoured by him
That the sun cooled
For black-eyed seconds
We gazed
The world was his
And he knew it

RH

❧ Weskus ☙

cosmic expanses echo
in the quarry
hello, hello, hello
the dog barks, barks, barks

clouds crouch
throwing shadows
into a hooded lizard eye ball

I lay low with daisies
a peeling garden gnome
mastering the art of skinning a bokkom

in two days
I'll see the city
and not even notice
the sky
or
my shadow's reverberation

NR

ՉՅՑ

small fish swims frantic
a Siamese fighter feeds
survival is fierce

NR

& Elephant &

low melodious rumble
　　delicate crackling of branches
black cutout
　　on soundless silver riverbed
the sly moon
　　impales him
number 31 honoured
　　as DH Lawrence
by his snake
　　the fence sizzles
five plops and a shower
　　fresh dung
leavening cold Scotch
　　an adjustment of shadow
a grassy gust
　　sibilance of frogs and cicadas
in the thickening dark
　　goodnight
　　　　　　　good night

RH

ಹ Nat Geo ಣ

Who made Jaguar?
Who watched Jaguar?
Who killed Jaguar?

And did you pursue the jaguar?

Brown bear in the snow.
People marvel and take photos.
Remember this, remember this.
Creatures, always do.

Jack-Ass penguin,
so proud.
You have more to crow about
than we.

A baby –
baby tiger, baby acorn,
ancient dog.

You soap your child,
all those hurts.

Once this world they say
was humanless.

Once wind ruled,
and grasses.

We are blessed to be
the least wondrous of all,
the ones who made the world,
who fought and raped it.

I come from this place unbearable,
unfettered by absolutes,
unsure even of my room.

Am I the Jaguar?

Lost to mystery,
but waiting.

JvN

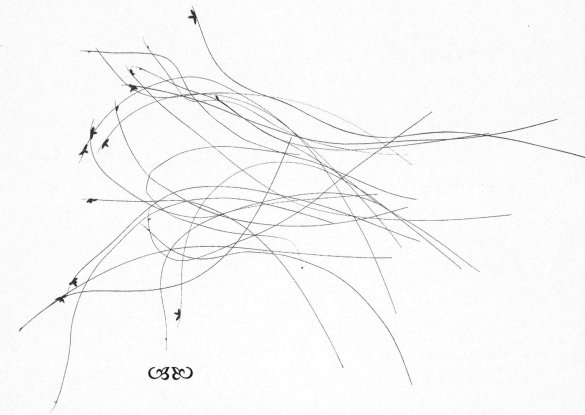

༄༅

crooked old blue gum
twisted arms and fingers hold
the infants till flight

NR

❧ Featherfangs, flowerthorns, whisperhorns ❧

Eerste river breaks her waters
consecrated drums offer long, hard groans
down her treacherous curves

gifts are exchanged with those
who have spoken
into early soaked hours

           *

sun rustles the bulrushes
bamboo reclines in the warmth
birds inspecting the reeds for
their young and eggs
a long black snake seeks the same

unfamiliar wetland
giving your
lifeless armored beetle
splayed desiccated frogs
sacrificed at the front door

each day reciting
endurance makes for surviving

gyrate with the lightning

NR

❧ The night-feeder ❧

Sunshine.

Bees are Ancients,
every leghair on my body tells me so.
But they know nothing of love,
I see that now.

You fine suckling flower,
your breath of cocaine and delicious violets,
satin velvet cashmere and blue
womb eyes
baby pod.
You came running out of me
and pulled me closer like a lollipop.

Your humorous diamond sky
lopsided smile
lake-like
the warmth from your body
ambient angel breath,
you fill me like apples.

We do the walk of love.

Child in the garden –
ancient, wonderful,
damply lipping me as Van Gogh
sails by.

I hear your breathing,
it is the sound of whales.

You beautiful breakfast baby,
pickled foot and bottom,
you coughed that bathwater
out like sea.

Picked by a cavalry of angels,
this lily that grew in the field
in aching delicacy.
But I did,
I did,
and they were softer than I thought.

JvN

134

൭ഌ

stream of swift soldiers
amass an autumn harvest
gifts for their ant queen

NR

ɞ Waterhole 03

In a cocoon of scalding sand
a hyena lies dying
filmy eyes brimming
with the den of babies
she's birthed and raised

they approach one by one
from a bend in the crusty riverbed
nudge her gently
before drinking from the pool
into which she drags herself

on the third day
eyes closed
ears flat
she is abandoned
indifferent to her vanished den
to the pitiless glare of the afternoon sun
the coming night
to enemy and prey alike

doves swoop in a soft clapping of wings
springbok twitch in stilt-legged perplexity
by the pool for a moment
then bend to drink
fleeing with the squirrels
as darkness skulks behind the dunes
makes bold
consumes her

RH

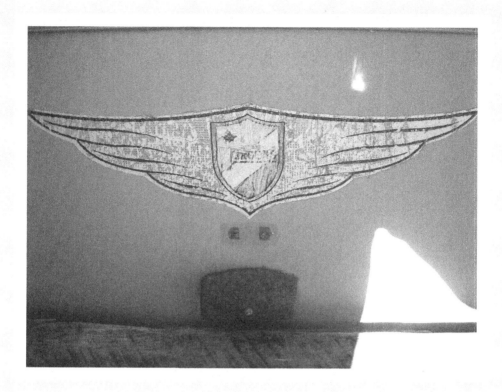

ଚ Travelling ଓ

a space we found
to fill
with silence
a detour
a route
of self sufficiency

a hopeful competence
that eventually discovered
a space under the brush
four footprints
your water bottle
my flint

NR

❧ Schism ☙

wind is changing
tectonic plates shifting

there's that trouble   a'bubbling
chaos we will be   a'raging
water walls we are   a'raising
arching
roaring
rolling out
spitting out

ash
    scum
        jagged jetsam

and then   silence
and then   peace

in the sunshine
on the shoreline
a collection of shells filled with sea chatter
a spiralled fog that will linger
on petrified wood and smoothed over sceptres

NR

ଓଞ୍ଚ

February morn
only the shade is moving
hot African buzz

NR

PASSAGES

જી8ৎ

sad poems in love's wake
bringing final acceptance
cooling a hot heart

જી8ৎ

summer charred with loss
autumn collection begins
winter's veil welcome

NR

❧ Love regained ☙

We started slow
words tangled
feelings inscribed on skin
used language without
caution unsuspecting
passionate as fools, believers and that
ilk
then it was over
life or something did it
things were never the same after that
I grieved for words log-jammed
in a separation of decades
our engravings mythical
as fine papyrus
until from God knows where
you came back
perhaps it was my yearning
you unspooled me
letter by letter
wound them around you
like a garland of petals
alluring mysterious
I swore never to let you go
or forget you in some dusty life

poetry my love

RH

❧ Beloved ☙

Your face rises from the mist
today rocks spill from you
your eyes like wild birds
creases on your brow

what troubles you
what storm skulks
beyond the horizon
of my vision

lying in wait
to fall upon the rocky
promontory
of your bones
gulls wheel above you

their disquiet
a canvas for your own
I have sensed your
every mood and kept my head

we are not so different
you and I
we have ventured
into the cave

felt the pounding of
its dark heart
tomorrow the sun will venture
in
the winds forswear violence

dolphins will return
to the chase
a whale will blow
you into a salty sky

and I?
I will look into
the mirror of your face
see there my reflection

RH

☙

greying roots reaching
insight strokes tired temples
softening the years

NR

❧ Lest I forget ☙

Is it winter
my winter
a tree from which no
leaf will ever
sprout again
the slow bark stripped
bare branches
beseeching the sky
a knotty thicket
of grey clinging
like the prickly nest of
parasitic birds
daily fattening
as words grow leaner

Words went first

dead leaves
fluttering singly
around me
I chased each word
but they turned to
misshapen things
bugs or roaches
I got down on my knees
picked them up
crunched them
between my palms
between my teeth
swallowed them

Then I forgot the sunset

I forgot the shape of home
lost the names of my children
my husband
I forgot my own name
it slid off my tongue
I remembered how to write
I wrote it all down
all the names
the letters dropping
into my little black book
long lists
of everybody
and everything
daylight darkness
the scent of rain
a nameless melody
that makes me tremble
the word mountain
the word for salt water
I cannot find

Doctor knows about losing things

I remember somebody
who smiled a lot
a whiff of something
cigarettes says doctor
you smoked
thirty a day
gave it up years ago
a razor of light
or perhaps lightning
pierces the thicket
a word
young
so faint
I can barely say it

I consult my black book

baby
child
boy
girl
man
woman
the word sex
large easy
three letters

S-E-X

doctor laughs
points to a man
beside him

your husband
of forty-five years
the father of your children
what children
she's tired says doctor
are you tired?
I ask the stranger
with the shiny eyes

his smell dark and close
don't you know me Jane
yesterday you knew me
it's Mike your husband
please try
what is Mike?
I pick up my black book
shake my head
so many words
but I can't find Mike

RH

ೞ

green vine, not yet ripe
hue of sweet drunken promise
waits for love season

ೞ

humble gift haiku
succulent marrow of word
solid bone of mood

ೞ

the young geese have flown!
autumn skies, empty omen
we should move on soon

NR

❧ The Story Clouds ☙

These are a handful of notes in a difficult book,
they're slippery and quite insistent.

You know, I am a word, a colour,
I am not even afraid.

I saw a small bit of the night,
your heart like footsteps in the house.

Slung in the arms of trees
I'm afraid, I do it anyway:
Eternity.

Even though we will be parting
at the Blue Mountains
back into the black goodness
I will always be someone to you.

Yesterday I told you

I went to the Hothouse
without bibs or chains.
Thoughts of you (where you lay.)

A wolf ate the cold winter in my mind.

JvN

ʕ From God to dust* ʘ

In our sleep, pain that cannot forget falls drop
by drop upon the heart and in our despair,
against our will comes wisdom through the
awful grace of God.
- Aeschylus: Agamemnon

I

Emergency years.
Haas Das se Nuuskas.
More news at Seven, or as it happens.

God is in the dreadful things,
the small things,
the day they took all our furniture away.

It was time.

This house is a hundred years old.
And I have been congenitally unable to live.

I write in my little locker:
The Protest Poet,
running backwards and forewords
forwards and backwards
for words

and a poem for myself cannot be,
only that.

II

The things we don't talk about.
Your Domestic and the Law.
Eating in front of hungry people.

Oh god I am shrieking
top us gut us hang us out to dry!

The day Madam shat herself at the
Beauty Counter
in Stuttafords.
I tell you what,
the worst part was the smell,
sliding off gently.

When you don't believe that this is you,
when you don't believe
that this is mad
then Alice you have eaten me,
a shit sandwich,
a tin of fish's assholes.
And camels have green teeth.

Who did this to you, then?

Old men in Polyester,
a Bint who should know better,
the fatty lip on lamb.
The Competition.

Huddled like bananas,
we can do no more.
Even my day is wearing a seatbelt.

(They) have hidden
burnt boiled broken
all your Play Stuff –

these children,
these angry children
they drive Jettas, Astras and Scenics now.

Toyota.
Cambrio.

Quite a ride.

I do not know myself,
I lay wasted by my subterfuge.

III

"Maybe we'll come to understand
one another –"
this glorious existence,
a galaxy inside of me,
an Orchid,
and we wonder if there is a Love
Palm on their toilet.

This is a house that people live in.

I am a Parvenu.
I live on charity.
I renounce my individuality.

And
in fact
everything passes.

Everything is change,
nothing has changed,
the change bank,
the change lady,

it's all change,
it's been neglected for so long.

An Artemis,
always ready for the hunt,
hurt by accidental non-crimes.

This is an old house.

IV

And Peace, who is she?
The night of Divali,
The festival of Luxmi,

it sounds like something from a dream.

– only if you feel
what's right in front of you –

paradise came to me like this poem did,
in daywear.

I looked up and saw it

light

The fallen angel
his perfect shattering
so that we should see
what colour we were made.

JvN

---

* Words attributed to Swami Venkatesananda, who
visited District Six before it was demolished. This poem
was produced in response to a request for "A Protest
Poem for the New South Africa".

❧ Better ❧

I kiss you better
the sun filling the bay
against the nibbling small bit of your sanctity

and push my lips up against
all your pristine cheek
more and more
it will get better.

But life may end like this
that you never be better
that you never get better
than this.

And more and more
you may know yourself
the sucking ache
that is hanging you
to this lifetime.

So when your chance comes
take it you must
And though we are pressed against it
turn your cheek away from us
And though there are oceans in this,
cut us loose with a kiss.

JvN

❧ Courtship of eagles ☙

there are times
when I begin to speak
that my tongue is a moat
hemmed in on all sides
by teeth and eyes
by towers
of words as cumbersome
and unforgiving
as unspoken truths

there are times
when words flow wild
skim through walls
sweep aside boulders
ride the sky
as eloquent and soaring
as a courtship of eagles

RH

ೞ

sunshine births berries
patient basket pauses
for juicy red runners

NR

❧ Gentle journey ☙

I'd say high serotonin you lucky bugger
it wasn't enough
his organs fat with melanomas
giant toxic grapes
dodging sliding
beneath scalpels
of Sloan Kettering surgeons
birthing offspring
in tributaries of blood
deposited on malignant islands
of failing organs.

The luckless bones of his skull
melting from sinister drugs
Rosebud, he says
I'm good for the hospice.

I won't see you before I go
I hope for a painless journey.

Hold thumbs.

RH

❧ Via Appia ☙

"the Appian way is the queen of the long roads"

How these poems were born:
shot crows
loose words
broken crystals
the dreadful baby.

First at the hill is some man
jogging with his elegant calves.

At the apex (I presume)
is tenderness.

Via Appia –
the first art
the first ornaments
the first status

It's the river delicious, I am clay again.

Water dripping off my chin,
with pork for brains and fish
more beautiful than jewellery.

Imagine if you can
a bird with no wings

the owls calling to me,
the toilet stall
the ozone of procrastination.

Hours, then days
in which I wish this hadn't happened to me.
The rock in my throat, saying
we're in it now.

We're in it now,
up in the cave where destiny could smote me
with its deadly smell.

Up in the cave with its bad smell
I endure what everyone wants:
to know a love like mine

to see its silt ways use me.

JvN

ഇ Boa Morte ര
(Song of Life)

I remember you when you were young and
vigorous.

This is life:
In the beginning
We all piss ourselves, it's not Austen.

We wake up rumpled, we are bald
Our feet are hoary.
The smell of haddock in the morning
The endless reshuffling of regrets and half-worn
garments.

This is not a place of fluffy handtowels
We are not brave all the time
The exhausting breakfast
The nauseating smell of chicken in the morning
The hard and predictable road back –

It hurts like I am born.

The animal afraid of losing himself
This cupboard of my tiny life
It is this simple, so.

Tonight I just feel old.

Death is always calling me:
Be Aware. Write longer.
I mourn myself,
My death, my passing, while I can.

Life Without Me.

It hurts like I am born.

Man of the Cloth
Back on Hell's highway,
Dead like me –
Scared by fear.

You don't die easy, either.
Surrender the fight.

Either today tomorrow or later
We hear the silence of our sleep,
And I remember dying.

Repeat: refrain, refrain
I mourn my passing, while I can

Yes, that too
Yes, all of that

And even our faces change.

I remember you
smell like breakfast in a hotel
this cupboard of my tiny life
I am *Vivianne* Westwood
I am *Earnest* Hemingway
It doesn't really matter,
though I sometimes think it do.

Come back, come back

It's some way off but it's still there.
The worms will eat this flesh,
I do not love this flesh.
I tie my fate to yours.

By how much more can I make you
mine,
I tie myself to die.

I dressed like an orphan.
The light on the cupboard was like
silver leaves
Silver rocks on the black mountain
I drank my milk.
I washed my bum.
Boa Morte: set down this
I am not dissatisfied.

JvN

the
POETS

Jana van Niekerk studied English and Drama at UCT and holds a DPhil in Psychology from Stellenbosch University on the subject of Infant Observation. She worked as a stage, film and television actress, theatre director, and clinical psychologist before committing to writing full-time. Her poetry and short stories have appeared in various local and international literary journals, in print and online. She lives in Scarborough with her partner, her children and her dog. She is writing her first novel.

Rosemund Handler holds an MA in Creative Writing from UCT and has written four novels, all published by Penguin. Her poetry and short stories have been published in various journals and anthologies. Her favourite poet is probably Ted Hughes, but she also enjoys reading and admiring the work of many other poets.

Natalie Railoun moves in and out of the sun; she has lived all her life on the Cape Peninsula, been subject to its days of glory and its storms; she knows its peoples intimately and has clear vision with regard to the contours and colours of their souls; she has two boys and a husband; loves others, too; writes poems to extract the essence of all she feels and compounds into thought; Natalie is delicate and yet proven robust; Helderberg is her region.